D1755136

PEN TO PAPER

— THIS BOOK BELONGS TO —

PEN TO PAPER

A PERSONAL NOTEBOOK

ILLUSTRATIONS BY
HENRIETTE WILLEBEEK LE MAIR

GALLERY & PEN TO PAPER PRODUCTS
LONDON AND THE HAGUE

THE BEAUTIFUL AND EVOCATIVE
ILLUSTRATIONS IN 'GOLDEN DAYS' ARE
THE WORK OF THE DUTCH ARTIST
HENRIETTE WILLEBEEK LE MAIR (1889-1966).

SHE WAS THE DAUGHTER OF A
WEALTHY MERCHANT WHO HAD AN INTEREST
IN ART AND ENCOURAGED HER TO PAINT AND
DRAW FROM AN EARLY AGE.

PUBLISHERS WERE ATTRACTED BY HER
DELICATE AND DETAILED DRAWINGS AND
HER FEELING FOR DECORATION AND
MISS LE MAIR WAS COMMISSIONED TO
ILLUSTRATE SEVERAL CHILDREN'S BOOKS
WITH RHYMES BETWEEN 1911-1926.

MANY OF THE ILLUSTRATIONS IN
'GOLDEN DAYS' ARE FROM THIS PERIOD
SHOWING THE ARTIST'S ABILITY TO CAPTURE THE
SPIRIT OF CHILDHOOD WITH HER DELIGHTFUL
PORTRAYALS OF YOUNG PEOPLE.

ILLUSTRATIONS COPYRIGHT © 1991

BY SOEFI STICHTING INAYAT FUNDATIE SIRDAR.
PUBLISHED BY GALLERY CHILDREN'S BOOKS
AN IMPRINT OF EAST-WEST PUBLICATIONS (UK) LIMITED
8 CALEDONIA STREET, LONDON N1 9DZ

ALL INQUIRIES TO EAST-WEST PUBLICATIONS.
PRINTED AND BOUND IN HONG KONG
BY SOUTH CHINA PRINTING COMPANY.
ISBN 0 85692 196 3
FIRST IMPRESSION
THE TEXT AND ILLUSTRATIONS WITHIN THIS BOOK
ARE COPYRIGHT UNDER THE BERNE CONVENTION.
NO PART MAY BE REPRODUCED, STORED IN A
RETRIEVAL SYSTEM OR TRANSMITTED IN ANY WAY
WITHOUT PRIOR PERMISSION OF THE COPYRIGHT
OWNERS, NOTWITHSTANDING FAIR DEALINGS FOR
THE PURPOSES OF REVIEW AS PERMITTED BY THE
COPYRIGHT ACT 1956.